A Writer's

An A to Z of ideas and information on the art and craft of creative writing

Lindsay Stanberry-Flynn

Copyright © Lindsay Stanberry-Flynn 2013

The moral right of the author has been asserted.

Apart from any use permitted under UK copyright law, this publication may only be reproduced, stored or transmitted, in any form, or by any means with prior permission in writing of the publishers in accordance with the terms of licences issued by the Copyright Licensing Agency.

Green Shoots Publishing

A Writer's Alphabet

*An A to Z of ideas and information
on the art and craft of creative writing*

Lindsay Stanberry-Flynn

Green Shoots Publishing

For the interesting and talented

creative writing students

I've taught

Table of Contents

Introduction	1
Anxiety	3
Books and Brains	5
Creating Characters	9
Dreams	13
Enervate	17
Feedback and Facebook	19
Goals	25
Hook	27
Ideas and Indie (publishers)	31
Journey	39
Kettles	43
Love	47
Marketing	53
Nothing	55
Openings	59
Plot	63
Questions	69
Rejection	73
Secrets, Shadows and Suspense	77
Titles	81
Unravelling	85
Voice and Viewpoint	89
Write	93
X-Ray	97
Yellow	101
Zenith	105
Acknowledgements	107
About the author	109

Introduction

The idea for this book was inspired by a blogging challenge I undertook in 2012. Hitting a low patch in my writing, I needed to inject some new impetus to stir the creative juices.

I'd read about other blogging challenges and decided that I would write a series of posts, one each day, based on the alphabet, and that they would be connected to an aspect of creative writing – its highs and lows, achievements and challenges, its rewards and disappointments.

Some of the posts related to key features of the craft of writing, such as creating characters, plotting and openings. Others were more random topics, for example the importance of kettles to a writer and why it's essential to know the precise meanings of words.

The blogging challenge proved successful for me. When the twenty-six days were over, I found I had written over 15,000 words, when before I was struggling to write anything. Better still, I'd enjoyed the challenge and felt motivated to return to my stalled novel. The task of writing something every day suddenly didn't seem to be such a hurdle. The blog had got me back on track.

A number of people who read my blog said how much they'd enjoyed the posts and urged me to turn them into a book. *A Writer's Alphabet* is the result! It's a book about writing – and there are already more of those than a potential writer could manage to read. But this offers a personal, somewhat quirky, glance into writing and a writer's life that I hope can be enjoyed by both writers and anybody interested in the process of producing fiction.

Lindsay Stanberry-Flynn

A

Anxiety

It feels to me as if anxiety is the accompanying music to a writer's world.

- Have I got any ideas? What can I write about?
- Have I got anything interesting, worthwhile, or new to say?
- I'm frightened of the blank white page.
- I've got an idea, but can I make it work? The idea is strong and secure while it's in my head, but it disintegrates when I try to put it into words.
- This writing is rubbish. Why would anyone want to read it?
- Why am I wasting time sitting in front of a computer writing stuff that no one but me cares about when I could be seeing friends, walking by the river, gardening, reading, lying in a darkened room ...
- I've sent my story off to a competition, but I doubt it will get anywhere.
- Oh, it's made the shortlist, but it can't possibly win.

- I've finished the tenth draft of my novel, but will anyone want to publish it?
- Shall I self-publish? How will I sell it if I do?

On and on and on ... the voices chatter, question, churn the stomach. To write or not to write – when it involves such anxiety – that is the question!

B

Books and Brains

I didn't have to think too hard about this one! Reading has been an essential part of my life since I was a small child. My earliest memories of reading are the Noddy and Big Ears series, quickly followed by Enid Blyton's Famous Five Books. I used to go to the library every Saturday and take out four books – I seem to remember having finished them long before the week was up! I then moved on to books such as *Fourth Form at Mallory Towers* and *Sue Barton: Student Nurse* and can remember loving all the books in both series.

Around the same time, I read and loved *Heidi*, *Black Beauty* (read that over and over again) and *Little Women* together with the other three books in the series by Louisa M. Alcott. I think I got my early feminist ideas from the character Jo.

At school, we read Jane Austen, the Brontes, George Eliot, and I enjoyed all of them. My English teacher was mad about Jane Austen – she used to say that heaven would be finding out there was a stack of Jane Austens she hadn't read. I didn't read Eliot's *Middlemarch* until I was at college, when my English lecturer said it was *the* novel for *the* adult. Still not sure what he meant, but it sounds good! Dickens is one of the big names that I wasn't all that keen on, but it always seems heretical to admit that.

In my late teens and twenties I read people such as Thomas Hardy, DH Lawrence, Graham Greene, EM Forster, Alexander Solzenitsyn and Doris Lessing. I remember reading Greene's *The End of the Affair* and Rosamund Lehmann's *The Weather in the Streets* compulsively when romantic adventures didn't work out as planned! And thinking about doomed romances, I loved *Anna Karenina* and *Madame Bovary*. It was comforting to read about other people's pain - even fictional ones.

It took me a while to come to Virginia Woolf, but having done so, I really enjoyed her novels, although they're not easy reads. I got a lot out of reading her writer's diaries and gaining insight into her creative processes, her feminist thoughts in *A Room of One's Own*, and her essays, such as *Mr Bennett and Mrs Brown* where she explores the importance of creating believable rounded characters. Some years ago, I visited Woolf's home in Sussex, Monk's House, and Charleston farmhouse where her sister, Vanessa Bell lived with a brood of children and artistic visitors. The contrast between the two homes - one barren and ascetic, the other colourful and exuberant -

is a fascinating insight into their lives.

So, on to my second topic for B: Brains
I find first drafts incredibly difficult. What I'm writing feels like rubbish – clunky, clichéd, full of telling, repetitive, over-written, under-written … the list is endless. To let these things go and simply write is painful.

The problem is the left brain, the part of the brain that we use for so many tasks. In the modern world, it seems as if we're conditioned to let this side of the brain dominate at the expense of the other side, when really both sides are necessary.

According to the theory of left-brain or right-brain dominance (which emerged from the work of Roger W. Sperry into epilepsy), each side of the brain controls different types of thinking.

The left-brain, right-brain dominance theory puts forward the idea that the right side of the brain is better at expressive and creative tasks, while the left brain is thought to be more logical, analytical, objective, critical, dealing with order and structure. It controls all the areas that spell death to a writer's fledgling visions.

This means that at the first draft stage of creating, the right brain, dealing with intuition, emotion, imagination, creativity, needs to be given free rein. If the left brain is allowed a look-in, then doubts and insecurities inevitably surface. The imagination has to be given permission to create without fear of judgement, censure or mockery.

This stage is what Roz Morris in her book *Nail Your Novel* describes as **guided dreaming:** *Your dreaming brain doesn't get stuck. It's a private experience; it doesn't have to please an audience. It explores and often surprises. There will be rubbish, but there will also be moments of sublime inspiration and crazy invention.*

Wise words. They make perfect sense: banishing the inner critic is essential if a writer is to have the freedom to explore and invent in a first draft. So, why, knowing this, do I find it so difficult to give myself permission to write rubbish?

C

Creating Characters

How do you make your characters real? How do you create a fictional representation of a person who is vivid, knowable, almost seeming to step off the page? How can you create characters who readers have no difficulty identifying with and caring about? You will know when you have as they are characters who seem almost autonomous, guiding the course of the plot, sometimes in surprising directions.

Real characters are born only when you know them inside and out. Outside knowledge means knowing a character's physical attributes and public persona. Inside knowledge means his or her private and personal side.

Outside knowledge: often the starting point for getting to know your characters. What do they look like? What is their biography? What star sign are they? What are their likes and dislikes? It is useful to write a profile of each main character, listing as many attributes as you can. Think about their past: what sort of school did they go to? Do they have brothers and sisters? What sort of upbringing did they have?

These are important formative influences on real people. If you want to create 'real' characters, they need a personality and a history.

Inside knowledge: far more important than the surface information is the knowledge of what sort of a person your character is. In life we make snap judgements all the time using outside knowledge as indicators. However, this first impression is often re-evaluated when we get to know someone. Who is this person really – the first impression or the person we see in action? The challenge for a writer is to show characters in action.

Robert McKee, the screenwriter, defines character as the choices we make under pressure. It is when people are put in challenging situations and make critical choices that they show their true colours. This is why conflict is at the heart of fiction.

You will understand your characters only when you know how they react under pressure. And you will know this only when you understand their motivation. What do they want? Everybody wants something in fiction: conflict arises when the things are mutually incompatible, or are not forthcoming.

A sentence to sum up the essence of a piece of fiction: [character] wants [goal] because [motivation] but [conflict] can help a writer achieve a clear sense of what a story is about. An example might be Mary Brown, an eighty-year-old virgin, wants to meet a man because she wants to experience sex at least once before she dies, but her advert in the local paper produces no applicants for the job.

Once a character emerges in a writer's mind, and the ground work to flesh them out is done (it's never completely done as it's an ongoing process where a writer is always 'growing' their character and learning more about them), plot ideas can be generated. The best plots come out of character.

A couple of simple examples which I often use with my writing students: two different characters jump a red light, are caught by police and fined. Character A accepts he/she was in the wrong, pays the fine, accepts the penalty points and the incident is closed. The sensible way to behave, but not very interesting from a fictional point of view. There might be more to be gained in story terms by Character B's actions. He/she denies they jumped the light, gets into an argument with the police, lashes out with their fists and is arrested. The same incident but with two different characters generates a different plot.

Secondly, two people, each on a diet, go into a coffee shop and are confronted by a chocolate éclair with cream oozing out of the pastry and a thick coating of chocolate on top. Character A remembers his/her diet, refuses to be tempted, orders a coffee and retreats to a table, halo intact. Character B gives in and eats the éclair, only to suffer guilt and regret.

In each case, the different character generates a different outcome. We understand characters when they 'do' things. This is why it's so important for writers to show their characters in action.

D

Dreams

Everyone dreams, but some people seem to remember them much more vividly than others. Or, at least, they enjoy recalling and describing them. I prefer nights when I'm not aware of my dreams, when I go to sleep and wake up the next morning without the disturbance of this 'other' world.

And yet, I recognise that dreams are important. Our conscious selves wear masks. We greet the world (and often ourselves) with a veneer that conceals much of who we really are. The subconscious is rarely allowed to make its voice heard. But through dreams, the submerged, often ignored, layers of our personality – rich and multi-dimensional – can live. Plato said 'The unexplored life is not worth living.'

There's no doubt that dreams are a source of creativity, literature and discoveries. We have all experienced waking in the night with a brilliant idea, which if not written down, will usually have fled by the morning. We've all gone to bed thinking about a problem, a difficulty we need to resolve, only to wake up the next morning with the answer in our heads.

It's surprising how often dreams are a mishmash of things that have happened during the day. Clearly they help us sort through the debris, collating, absorbing, rejecting.

Then there are the nightmares. Those painful dreams when you find yourself falling, unable to move, in distress of some kind. Years ago, when I was going through a painful period of my life, I dreamt constantly of a house. It was always the same house – huge with loads of rooms. But I could never decide which room would have which function. There was nowhere to settle in this house. I used to rush from room to room, trying to work out if it should be a sitting room or a bedroom, and never being able to decide. Every time I dreamt about the house, I had to go through the same torment. I didn't need to be told by Freud – 'dreams are the royal road to the unconscious' – to work out the psychological significance of the dream.

Dreams play a huge part in literature, being used to reveal a character's psychological state: 'When Gregor Samsa woke up one morning from unsettling dreams, he found himself transformed in his bed into a monstrous vermin.' (Kafka *Metamorphosis*) and 'I sometimes dream of devils. It's night, I'm in my room, and suddenly there are devils everywhere. In all the corners and under the table, and they open doors, and behind the doors there are crowds of them, and they all want to come in and seize me. And they are already coming near and taking hold of me, But suddenly I cross myself and they draw back, they are afraid, only they don't go away, but stand near the door and in the corners, waiting.' (Dostoevsky *The Brothers Karamazov*).

Dreams have also generated stories or been the stimulus for novels. In 1816, Mary Shelley was eighteen years old when she spent the summer with her lover (and future husband) Percy Shelley, at Lord Byron's estate in Switzerland. One night, as they sat around the fire, the conversation turned to the subject of reanimating human bodies using electrical currents. Shelley went to bed that night with images of corpses coming back to life swirling through her head; as she slept, she clearly saw Frankenstein's monster and imagined the circumstances under which he had been created. Next morning she wrote a short story which she later turned into the novel *Frankenstein*.

In 1960, Jack Kerouac published *Book of Dreams*, an experimental novel, based on the dream journal he kept from 1952 to 1960. In it Kerouac tries to continue plot-lines with characters from his books as he sees them in his dreams.

I suppose the message for a writer, or anyone who wants to tune into their creativity, is – keep dreaming, dream big, use your dreams. So I guess I'd better let go of my 'quiet nights'. Bring on the dreams!

E

Enervate

You're probably thinking: What's this all about? What a weird word to choose when there are topics such editing and endings. Those subjects are important, but they do get an airing elsewhere in the book, and there is a writing-related reason behind this strange choice.

The dictionary definition of enervate is *wanting in (physical, moral, literary, artistic) vigour.* What! Only the fifth letter of the alphabet and I'm flagging. I'll never get to Z at this rate.

But I haven't chosen the word because it describes my current state, but because at one time, I used to think it meant the exact opposite! I came home from something one day – a workshop, a meeting, a day out (can't remember the circumstances) and wrote in my diary 'Had a fantastic day. Feeling completely enervated.'

What an idiot! I meant exhilarated, stimulated, excited, and I managed to come up with a word meaning the complete opposite.

That's an extreme example, but it helps show what pesky little things words can be.

Sometimes, you think you know the meaning of a word, but if you're asked to define it, can't do so precisely. Or you find that it doesn't mean **quite** what you thought it did.

Words are a writer's tools. They are wonderful, magical things that can help you create people, places, stories. They can produce gold dust. Or they can produce dross. Generally, though, it helps if you know what they mean!

'Words are sacred. They deserve respect. If you get the right ones, in the right order, you can nudge the world a little.' Tom Stoppard

F

Feedback and Facebook

Feedback on our writing is essential for two reasons. One, we are too close to our work. However much we strive for objectivity, however long we put away a piece of writing to try to come back with fresh eyes, it is still **our** work. We created it. It's our baby – imagine looking at your 'real' baby and thinking *Ugh! You're ugly*! Not impossible, but hard to do.

Two, when we write, we are clearly thinking as writers immersed in the mechanics of character creation, plot, structure, dialogue – the list is endless. It is often easy to forget about our reader: that precious person we want and need to read our words, engage with our characters and feel moved by our stories.

We have to ask the reader: *how is it for you?* This is where the value of feedback comes in. But it's probably best not to ask your mother (who loves you) or friends, at least those without some understanding of what makes a piece of writing work and what doesn't. A trusted writing group can be invaluable in getting some perspective on work before it reaches a wider audience. There are a number of companies and individuals who offer critique services. However, it's important to do some research on whoever it is you're trusting to comment on your work to make sure they are professional and give value for money. Critiques are not cheap, but they can pay dividends.

Giving feedback on other people's writing can be a useful process. As a creative writing tutor, I've read hundreds of chapters from novels, stories, poems, and I've learnt a lot from the experience. It is easier to spot the 'saggy' bits of a story, or a character who fails to come alive, or an unconvincing plot in someone else's work. Identifying such areas can be helpful when reviewing one's own writing. However, giving feedback must be handled with sensitivity. Natural protective mechanisms mean harsh, brutal criticism can be destructive and impossible for the writer to work with.

Once a book is published, the question of feedback through reviews occurs. This used to be the province of professional reviewers in journals and newspapers. Now the process has become much more democratic with the advent of Amazon's review system. These reviews on Amazon, as well as on internet sites such as GoodReads and various book bloggers can be vital to the success or otherwise of a new or unknown author, especially the 4 and 5 star variety. Authors crave them. However, potential readers have to take into account that a percentage of these reviews might have been written by friends or family of the author. Sometimes, it seems, even famous authors will go to any lengths to amass rave reviews on Amazon, even adopting different personae so that they can post favourable reviews for their **own** books!

But, perhaps, the sweetest reviews for me come when a reader, previously unknown to me, gets in touch to say how much they've enjoyed my novel. I'm immensely grateful for this feedback and touched that people have taken the time and trouble to write. I have to confess that I have never written to an author to tell them how I felt about their book, even if I loved it. But now I realise how rewarding it is when people do.

My second topic for F: Facebook
I arrived late at the Facebook party. I kept hearing that it was good fun, you could post photos, and it was an essential networking tool and internet presence for writers nowadays. I wasn't too worried about the first two, but the last one did interest me.

However, I resisted it for ages on the grounds that it would waste time and it would increase my already highly developed tendency to procrastinate. I was afraid I would have less time for writing.

Those fears *have* come true. When my writing isn't going well (and sometimes even if it is going very well), I think *I'll just have a quick look at FB* – emails fulfil the same function. It's amazing the amount of time it's possible to spend 'amusing' oneself reading other people's posts. And sometimes a rash of commenting and liking breaks out. I don't know why, but the drive to comment and like seems to come in waves.

So, the downside is significant, but what I hadn't fully appreciated were the positives. I have made a huge number of writing contacts through FB, have found out about events and opportunities and feel much more in touch with other writers.

I've got an author page, where I try to post writing news and activities. But I'm also conscious that people who go on FB simply to 'boast' don't win many fans. Recognising other people's achievements and news matters, and it's encouraging to see how supportive writers are of each other's successes (and 'downs'). It's also nice to post things that might be of interest to others. The etiquette of it all is as finely balanced as etiquette in ordinary life.

There is also a lot of fun to be had. Some of the pictures and cartoons people post have made me laugh out loud, and it's entertaining to see people's responses and join in the 'conversation'. Recently there was a thread which asked for film titles where the word 'bacon' took the place of one of the original words in the title. There were some funny offerings, and I was pleased with my *The Devil Wears Bacon* and *The French Lieutenant's Bacon*!

There *are* some worrying aspects about putting stuff about yourself out there into the ether, and I'm wary of giving too much personal information. But so much of our lives in on record nowadays anyway that it probably doesn't make much difference.

G

Goals

Modern life seems to be all about to-do lists and achieving. You have to have priorities; you need aims; you must have goals, so we're told.

Often goals are set for us by parents, or teachers, and later on by those above us at work. Before you even get the job, the interviewing panel are likely to ask, 'Where do you want to be in five years?'

Sometimes your partner in life might suggest goals: 'We've got to set aside an evening a week to spend together.' Or you might set goals for yourself: you want to lose weight, or run in the London Marathon next year, or trek through the Amazon rainforest.

But more often than not, I suspect, most of us are happy to get to the end of the day, the end of the book we're reading, the end of the bottle – no, that last one is probably **not** a good example! But, realistically, the majority of people are not overly ambitious. Human nature being all too often disposed towards apathy and procrastination, many of us tend to drift.

However, such sloppiness in not good enough for characters in fiction. An essential part of their raison d'être is a goal. It might be big – the terminally ill person who wants to visit the States before it's too late, or small – the person on a diet who longs for a piece of chocolate, but the yearning has to exist and it has to be thwarted. The character must have something they WANT, and something must stop them getting it.

There's a cliché that you only find out what people are really like in a crisis. If that's partly true in real life, it's completely true in fiction. Characters have to face conflict and through that, change – of some kind – occurs.

Here are a few characters and their goals. What conflict would you put in their way?

- Jodie is a forty-year old architect who is fed up drawing plans for modern boxes and wants to design something exciting and innovative.
- Fliss is twenty-five. She's been saving in secret for a trip to Australia because she thinks her biological father lives there.
- Josh was involved in a major car accident. His left leg has been amputated above the knee. He makes his mind up to compete in the paralympics in Rio.

Character + goal/motivation + conflict = plot. Easy!

H

Hook

In case you're worrying that this anthology has strayed from reading and writing to something more pugilistic, I'm not talking about a right hook but a narrative hook!

In today's crowded, frenetic world, it's hard to gain people's attention in any sphere, let alone fiction. Readers have got millions of things to do, and if a writer can't persuade them quickly that the book/story has something that makes it worthwhile for them to read on, then they will soon move onto their list of other-more-interesting-activities.

The literary technique for grabbing readers is known as a narrative hook. Interest your readers, intrigue them, puzzle them, delight them – *what* and *how* you do it doesn't really matter – but you have to give readers something that says to them *you won't regret investing your time in this book.*

A common method for hooking a reader is to ask a question. This can be either explicit or implicit, but it needs to come near the beginning, if not the first sentence then at least the first paragraph in a short story, or the first pages in a novel. The reader will then continue reading in order to learn the answer to the question.

It might be a huge question such as 'can this virus be stopped from wiping out humanity?' which could take the whole book to answer. Or it might be a smaller question, such as 'will the character give in to the temptation to eat the slice of birthday cake?' This might be answered quickly, but often unmasks other and bigger questions 'why is he/she trying to resist?' 'Will he/she succeed in dealing with the marital problems caused by over-eating?' 'What is he/she hiding from by indulging their appetite?'

The question hook done well is successful and effective. Reel us in (here, I'm counting myself as a reader) and we'll search for an answer. It doesn't matter if the answer takes a long time to come. In the most successful writing, that initial question isn't answered until the end of the book/story. But when it does come, it must satisfy the reader emotionally, psychologically and intellectually.

In other words, the answer to the question has **a lot** of work to do.

Sometimes the quality of the writing might be the hook – it might seduce a reader, so that he/she will read on without an obvious hook. This also applies to an interesting character or unusual setting. But through some means, that **hook** needs to be there.

Here are a few openings to see the 'hooks' and analyse how effective they are:

'No one had seen her naked until her death.' *The Birth of Venus* Sarah Dunant

'We slept in what had once been the gymnasium.' *The Handmaid's Tale* Margaret Atwood

'It was a bright, cold day in April, and the clocks were striking thirteen.' *1984* George Orwell

'There should be a scar.' *Unravelling* Lindsay Stanberry-Flynn

'Each year there was an outbreak of fever at the House of Orphans.' *House of Orphans* Helen Dunmore

'For a temporary shorthand-typist to be present at the discovery of a corpse on the first day of a new assignment, if not unique, is sufficiently rare to prevent its being regarded as an occupational hazard.' *Original Sin* PD James

I wonder which hooks you think work and why?

I

Ideas and Indie (publishers)

When I talk to readers about my writing, I am invariably asked – as I know other writers are – where I get my ideas from. In some ways it's an easy question. Ideas are everywhere: items in the newspaper, overheard conversations, photographs, finding something – one of my short stories *The Magic of Stories* involves a young woman finding a wedding ring in a ladies' cloakroom and her quest to find the ring's owner. That's why writers often carry notebooks with them, so that they can jot down ideas as and when they occur.

Sometimes writers wake up with an idea – the early morning before the conscious mind fully comes to life is often a fruitful time. Or, an idea comes just as you're falling asleep, and the decision then is whether to get up and make a note of it, or try to cling onto it in the hope that you'll remember it in the morning. I'm sure some of my best ideas have been lost by over-reliance on that latter method!

Other times, ideas remain stubbornly absent. You want to write, but nothing occurs to write about. Then it becomes necessary to work harder at it. Ask 'what if' questions; imagine intriguing situations, pushing things as far as they will go; put potential characters into situations involving conflict. Or you could take a walk in the park and pick something to write about: two boys playing football; a woman chasing a dog; a couple having an argument; a ball rolling down a hill. We are surrounded by possibilities for stories, but sometimes we have to dig to find them.

Writing prompts given in workshops or writing groups can also be useful in stimulating the imagination. In my writing group, we take turns to bring along an exercise for everyone to do. Sometimes it's hard to make the ideas come to order, but, nevertheless, everyone writes seriously for fifteen to twenty minutes, and it's astonishing to discover what you and others have created under this sort of pressure.

My second topic for I: Indies.
Indie publishers is another term for self-publishers, those people brave, mad or misguided enough to publish their own books. And there are plenty in each of those categories!

More and more writers are following this path, especially since technology made it possible and affordable for 'ordinary' people, and since the guards at the entrance to the inner sanctum of mainstream publishing became ever more dismissive of those hammering at the doors.

Until a few years ago, self-publishing had a bad name being equated with vanity publishing, where companies take a lot of money to print only a few copies of a book, with no intention of marketing or promoting it. Such books rarely reach many readers.

Jonathan Clifford, who is credited with coining the phrase in 1959, and who has written vociferously on the subject says 'A dishonest vanity publisher makes money not by selling copies of a book, but by charging clients as much as possible to print an unspecified number of copies of that book. Some vanity publishers will print as few copies as they feel they can get away with.'

But before the arrival of commercially-driven vanity publishers, self-publishing had had a long and noble history. Writers whose names we are all familiar with are known to have self-published at some time in their career. People such as Gertrude Stein, Ezra Pound, Bernard Shaw, Virginia Woolf, Rudyard Kipling, Margaret Atwood, Stephen King, DH Lawrence. And books that were originally self-published include *Ulysses* by James Joyce, *Peter Rabbit* by Beatrix Potter, *The Bridges of Madison County* by

Robert James Walter, one of the best-selling books of the 20th century, *The Celestine Prophecy* by James Redfield who sold 100,000 copies from the boot of his car before a publisher agreed to publish it, and *Time to Kill* by John Grisham.

It took me a long time to come to self-publishing. I had always believed that if you were good enough, you would eventually be published. So, I kept writing novels, sending them off to agents and publishers (in those days publishers would accept unsolicited manuscripts) and often received an encouraging response. One agent almost took my fourth novel on, and Virago wrote 'We are sorry to be saying no to this.'

So, I hung on and believed that one day I would get there. Increasingly though, I began to realise that although more and more people were writing – as computers made it easier, and writing courses and groups sprung up all over the place – not many first novels seemed to be getting published. With the abolition of the net-book agreement in 1997, an agreement between the publishers and booksellers, which fixed the price at which a book could be sold, supermarkets and discount stores were able to sell copies of best-sellers at hugely-discounted prices. By 2009, 500 independent bookshops had closed. The advent of Amazon added fuel to the fire.

Publishers increasingly only wanted books that would be sure-fire successes. They would continue to publish their 'big' names and celebrities. Not only was it almost impossible for new writers to get published, but numbers of relatively successful writers (who were not bestsellers) were dropped by publishers. Writers such as Ian Rankin and Philip Pulman did not sell in huge numbers at first. It seems doubtful that publishers would continue to support them nowadays.

Of course, debut novelists still get published – some even achieve the heady heights of the Booker shortlist (*The Lighthouse* Alison Moore 2012) – but the numbers are miniscule, and there are a lot of very good writers whose work readers would enjoy who are not being given the chance.

As a result of all this, I decided – after a lot of heart-searching – to self-publish my novel *Unravelling*. I believed in it – I had written the first draft while I was doing my MA in creative writing at Bath Spa where Tessa Hadley was my manuscript tutor. I was no longer a novice – *Unravelling* is the sixth novel I've written. I paid to have an in-depth critique done on it; and I'd rewritten it several times, constantly improving and strengthening it.

I'm so pleased that I did self-publish. I've sold a respectable number of copies, a lot of people have told me how much they've enjoyed it (including strangers who had no need to pander to my ego, but who emailed with lovely comments); it's won three awards – winner of both the Chapter One Promotions Book Award and the Wishing Shelf Independent Book Award, and second in the 2011 Rubery International Book Award for books self-published and published by small presses. And I've had enormous fun and satisfaction.

I do believe there's an issue with people rushing work into publication which is either not ready, or simply isn't well-written enough to be published. This seems to be especially so with the ease with which people can now publish ebooks. Doubts about the quality of some of them don't help the case for quality indie publishers.

But, overall, they can't detract from the relevance, the importance and the power of self-publishing today. Mainstream publishing seems determined at the moment to keep its gates firmly shut, but soon the weight pushing against them will become overwhelming. They might then long for self-publishers to join them. But by then indie writers might say: 'Who cares? We don't need you.' Indeed, some are already committed to self-publishing and wouldn't even consider trawling the agents' lists.

My next novel *The Piano Player's Son* has a

small press publisher (Cinnamon Press 2013) but after that, who knows? I certainly would embrace self-publishing again!

J

Journey

When you set out to write a novel, you start on an amazing journey. It's a journey that will be rewarding, difficult, tiring, exciting, frustrating. You will find it challenging – intellectually, psychologically, emotionally, socially, and in many ways, physically. It's a journey that you will often consider abandoning – in fact a lot of people do give up and return 'home'.

If you make it through to the end, it will feel the most fantastic achievement. Even if you know your novel is not the greatest, finishing it will still provide a sense of elation. And you will be changed by the experience. You can't go through such an endeavour with all its highs and lows, ups and downs, without being changed. The end will be wonderful, a cause for celebration, but as is often the case, the destination is not as important as the journey itself.

And you are not the only one who will be changed. When you write a novel (or a short story), you create characters, people you will live with for months, if not years. And you will also send each of your main characters off on a journey. 'The task of the writer is to create characters on the verge of change, characters that will, in some way, be unrecognizable by the end of the work. *Ripe* characters.' (*The Plot Thickens* Noah Lukeman)

So, a character in a novel is on a journey. That might be a physical journey, an emotional journey, or the journey might be symbolic. It might be a combination of these. A prime example of the function and significance of the journey in the novel is *Jane Eyre*. Bronte's novel is set in five different locations, and in each one, Jane has different experiences, which give her a new level of maturity, until she has journeyed from vulnerable to powerful.

The journey a writer gives a character might be no more than the realisation that:

their dislike of the colour green relates to being made to eat sprouts as a child

the noise in the attic is an echo of their own pacing footsteps in the bedroom below

they love the person they thought they hated

Or it might be a much more fundamental jolting of the psychological self; or a revelation that transcends everything the character has ever known; or something in their background that makes them hate/love themselves.

If you are writing a novel, you need to send

your characters on journeys that will challenge you as well as them. You're going to share this journey with them. It's a long, hard slog, and it needs to be fun and enthralling – enjoy the journey!

K

Kettles

Kettles?! This might seem a bizarre choice for a writer's anthology, but I chose it because when I'm writing, the kettle is my best friend. Cups of tea and coffee sustain me through hours spent in front of the computer. I love the whole ritual of filling the kettle, waiting for the water to boil, getting the mug ready, the trip back up the stairs to my study at the top of the house.

Some years ago (well, lots of years ago) I undertook a fast. It seems mad now, but (for various reasons) I decided I would only drink water, fruit and vegetable juice for seven days, with no food! Given that I can barely go an hour now without food of some kind, I've got no idea how I did it. And not only did I do seven days, but actually went on for eight! Not long into the fast, I found the fruit and vegetable juice reminded my taste buds too much of food – they made it more difficult, so in the end I only had water. The point about this diversion is that I was conscious of how much I missed the ritual of the kettle and the tea making. Of how much the kettle is an integral part of daily life.

History of the kettle (with thanks to Wikipedia)

The first kettles were used in ancient Mesopotamia for purposes other than cooking. But over time these artistically decorated earthenware containers became more frequently utilized in the kitchen. Original kettles were typically made of iron and were placed directly over an open flame. This practice originated in China. Travellers used the kettles in order to produce potable water for themselves.

The word *kettle* originates from Old Norse *ketill* 'cauldron'. The Old English spelling was *cetel* with initial *che* – as in 'cherry', Middle English (and dialectal) was *chetel*, both come (together with German *Kessel* 'cauldron') ultimately from Germanic *katilaz*, that was borrowed from Latin *catillus*, diminutive form of *catīnus* 'deep vessel for serving or cooking food', which in various contexts is translated as 'bowl', 'deep dish', or 'funnel'.

During the 18th Century, the English began to manufacture tea pots out of earthenware, quickly replacing it with silver as materials became available. According to madehow.com, the development of tea kettles was in direct correlation with the evolution of the modern stove.

In the latter part of the 1800s, at the height of

the industrial revolution, electric tea kettles were introduced as an alternative to stove top kettles. The first electric kettles had a warming chamber outside the water source, but this was soon adapted in favour of an internal warming apparatus.

Writing exercise involving a kettle
Recently in my writing group, one of the members brought along an idea to stimulate some writing. The idea was the opening line: *I spent the morning at Camden Market, looking for a kettle that didn't switch itself off*. Here's my attempt, written in ten minutes and unfinished:

What a waste of time, I decided, as I ranged over the array of kettles on show – shiny, matt, glass, opaque, black lids, red lids, big spouts, small spouts – the choice was endless. But one that didn't switch itself off? Nope. No. Not a hope. Not a chance.

Why the hell had I agreed to such a stupid errand? I was almost out of the door when I thought I'd better tell Josie where I was going. A peace-offering. We hadn't spoken for twenty-four hours, since she'd called me a *stupid prat*. It wasn't as if she'd ever liked the vase in the first place. It had been her mother's, and you'd think she'd be grateful to me for breaking it.

So, I made my peace-offering: 'Just going to the market, Josie!' I called up the stairs, ready to make my escape.

'Oh, while you're there ... '

What the hell! I only told her as a point of info, to be polite – not so she could provide me with a shopping list.

'What?' I shouted back. 'What do you want?'

'Can you get a kettle that doesn't ... '

'Okay.' I was relieved to be off the hook. It seemed an easy request, but now ... I stared round ... what a bloody stupid mission.

'Have you got a kettle that doesn't switch itself off?' I asked the stall holder.

He shook his head.

'Why not?'

'No call for it, mate.'

'But I've just called for it.'

The stall holder shook his head. 'Who'd want to stand over a kettle waiting for it to boil?'

*

And that's all I had time for, but it's a good point – why would anyone want the inconvenience of a kettle that doesn't switch itself off? Thinking up challenging questions and searching for answers are important aspects of creative writing.

L

Love

When people ask me what my novel *Unravelling* is about, I want to say love, but I can see the impending yawn (especially from some men) if I do, and the neat pigeonholing of the book as light romance.

And yet the book is about love – as are so many novels, stories, poems, plays. Different sorts of love – sexual, familial, patriotic, friendship – but love in some form or another is surely what drives us as human beings. Its pursuit, its lack, its fulfilment.

In the reading group guide for *Unravelling* I described **the background** to the novel:

I wrote *Unravelling* because I wanted to explore the concept of a love that survives a lifetime, despite separation, estrangement and betrayal. Its early title was *All That Remains* from the notion that whatever life throws at us, what counts in the end – what 'remains' – is love.

I was interested in the idea taken from Plato's *Symposium* that humans were once made up of two halves, one female, one male. The gods, out of jealousy, split them in two, and now we spend our lives looking for our other half, our 'soul mate'. It's an idea that's prevalent in modern culture and perhaps an ideal we all yearn for.

When I read an article about someone's parents who remarried aged fifty-eight and seventy-three, having first eloped in the 1960s, the love affair at the heart of *Unravelling* was born.

Unravelling is different because it explores the contrasts between 'young' love and 'old' love, between passionate, dangerous love and quiet, secure love. It considers the forces that shape love at different times in our lives. While it is a novel about love, with a powerful love affair, passionate characters and an involving plot, it is not a romantic novel in the accepted sense.

Romance is a word frequently derided, especially in literature:

Oh no, I don't read romance – all that soppy mush. I like thrillers or science fiction.

Give me a crime novel or an adventure – can't be doing with love stuff.

are some of the comments people make about love stories.

But why? Surely love, falling in love, falling out of love, who we love, who loves us is crucial to human existence. It certainly plays a significant part in the happiness or unhappiness of our lives. And if one of the reasons why we read novels is to gain understanding of what it means to be a human being – to explore experiences and emotions we might share with the characters – then romance is essential reading.

Perhaps predictable and clichéd love stories in some women's magazines have helped give romance a bad name. Or, perhaps melodramatic dialogue and situations in some romantic novels have contributed to the scorn often poured on romance.

Noah Lukeman in his book on writing a novel *The First Five Pages* says 'Melodramatic dialogue comes in innumerable forms and the most common is probably romantic. Many writers have a tendency to push love scenes over the edge, to translate strong feelings into strong dialogue. Almost always this is a mistake.' And he gives this sort of dialogue as an example:

> *Oh, Henry!*
> Oh, Margaret!
> *They ran into each other's arms and embraced for what seemed like an eternity.*
> *Oh, Henry, you know I've loved you so!*
> *Oh, Margaret! If only words could express my love for you!*
> *He picked her up and spun her around in the field of magical, glowing dandelions.*

Most of us reading that would throw the book across the room and resolve never to pick up another romance. But there are some beautiful love stories. I remember crying over *The End of the Affair* by Graham Greene, and I loved Rosamund Lehmann's *The Weather in the Streets*. I've recently finished Helen Dunmore's *The Betrayal*, a sequel to *The Siege*. The novels describe the terrible events of the Siege of Leningrad during the Second World War and the brutal Stalinist years that followed, but at their heart is an exquisite love story which keeps the characters' humanity alive.

The blurb for *Unravelling* describes it *exploring the complexity and contradictions of love and sexual attraction,* which brings us to the tricky subject of sex! No romantic novel can call itself that without some love scenes in it, and for a contemporary novel that will almost certainly include sex. Modern readers don't want the dot dot dot as the bedroom door closes. We only have to think of the Fifty Shades' phenomenon to recognise that.

But how to write love scenes that aren't slushy or cloying or pornographic? What words should writers use? Biological terms sound like a text book; euphemisms like cop-outs; pet names idiotic in the 21st century. Writing a love scene means losing your inhibitions. I teach creative writing and sometimes give students a sex scene to write. Most of them are incredibly nervous about the challenge, or can only approach it in a jokey way.

But sex scenes can't be avoided. Real people have sex, and characters in a novel who are supposedly in love, but never have sex won't have the necessary credibility to make their readers care about them. It's not easy, but becomes easier if a writer doesn't think about the sex as a separate activity – a hurdle they must jump. I think the love scene must grow out of the characters and their relationship. The sexual tension that exists between characters must be there before the writer gives them the chance to fulfil it.

M

Marketing

Sometimes it seems the only thing that matters these days is MARKETING.

You have to network, plug, sell, tell, promote … on and on … you have to be out there shouting from the rooftops: *Look at me! I'm here!* If you're a writer that means 'building an author platform'.

Writing, by its very nature, tends to be a solitary business, especially if you are a fiction writer. You create worlds and people, you give birth to them on the computer and hope that they live on the page. These worlds and characters often seem more real to you than the actual world you inhabit.

But then the book is finished. You have to say goodbye to these people you have lived with so closely for so long, but you love them – and you want other people to love them. But how can they love them if they don't know about them? And that's the rub! You have to leave your solitary state and tell people about your book. You have to build an author platform!

In earlier times, that was a simpler process. For a start the publisher did most of it for you. You'd go to the launch, do a few readings in draughty halls and silent libraries, and hope readers would find your book. But in the 21st century – that's not enough. There's TECHNOLOGY.

Recently I went to a talk organised by my local Society of Authors group by a career psychologist, Denise Taylor on 'Marketing Your Book in the 21st Century'. The significance of the topic was shown in the numbers of people attending – about 50 people crowded into a smallish room, when usually only 15-20 attend the meetings. The talk was very good – Denise spoke about promoting your book on Amazon, websites, promotional material, blogging, networking on Facebook and Twitter, videos on YouTube, virtual book tours – the list of possibilities is endless.

I came out energised and determined to do more, do better, do everything. However, what made me laugh was the remark I overheard afterwards in the car park from one elderly attendee to another: 'Do you know, I just can't be arsed! ' And sometimes I know how she feels.

The problem is you can spend all your time promoting – in some form or another – and not writing.

N

Nothing

We all know what the word 'nothing' means, but let's consult the dictionary anyway. The *Concise Oxford Dictionary* defines nothing as *No thing, not anything, nought.* Difficult to write a post about then, but the word 'nothing' is more complex than that.

The concept of 'nothing' has intrigued philosophers, mathematicians, scientists, linguists for centuries. Can there possibly be a state of nothingness? Can human beings imagine a void of nothingness?

Nothing comes from nothing (ex nihilo nihil fit) is a philosophical expression of a thesis first argued by Parmenides. It is associated with ancient Greek cosmology, such as presented not just in the work of Homer and Hesiod, but also in virtually every philosophical system – there is no time interval in which a world didn't exist, since it couldn't be created *ex nihilo* in the first place. The Greeks also believed that things cannot disappear into nothing, just as they can't be created from nothing, but if they cease to exist, they transform into some other form of being. Today the idea is associated with the laws of mass and energy.

The word 'nothing' runs through Shakespeare's plays. Perhaps its most famous use is when King Lear says to his daughter Cordelia, 'Nothing will come of nothing.' He means if she remains silent and fails to declare how much she loves him, she will receive nothing. In fact, the play goes on to demonstrate that although she continues to say nothing, something – a huge tragedy – does arise from 'nothing'. There are other examples where the word does indeed mean something: Hamlet: *nothing either good or bad, but thinking makes it so*; Antony and Cleopatra: *And there is nothing left remarkable/Beneath the visiting moon*; Midsummer Night's Dream: *The form of things unknown, the poet's pen? Turns them into shapes, and gives to airy nothing/A local habitation and a name.* And it's worth remembering that in Shakespeare's time, the word 'nothing' had a sexual connotation!

One of my reasons for picking the subject for the letter N (besides tangling myself in knots with the complexities of the concept), is that 'nothing' often seems to feature in a writer's psyche. 'I've written nothing,' we say. 'I've done nothing for weeks.' We fear the blank page, the expanse of whiteness that reflects so distinctly our lack of words. I think it was Rolf Harris who said 'You have to kill the white.'

And from the point of view of writing, I think it's true that 'nothing will come from nothing'. If the page persists in remaining blank, we are left with only regret or guilt, a sense of failure, or possibly most crushing of all, the death of our dreams.

We have to *kill the white*. We have to write 'something', no matter how futile, rubbishy, or banal our words might seem. Because once they are down on the page, once there is 'something' to work with, the possibility of all sorts of gold emerges.

If you want to write, you have to get words on the page; you have to put 'something' down. 'Nothing' is not an option!

O

Openings

Apparently a novel – if it's not by an author the reader already knows, or a classic which some readers will persist with even if they're not enjoying it – has four minutes to make its mark on the reader. 99% of readers will certainly have made up their mind by page five and they're not going to change it. And this applies if it's purchasing from a shop or borrowing from the library. The front cover must attract; the title must intrigue; the blurb must excite, and the first paragraph must sell it.

Wow! For a writer, that's scary. If I don't manage to entice the reader with the cover, blurb and first paragraph/page, then my book stays on the shelf. However, I recognise that for me, as a reader, the four-minute rule largely holds true.

So, how am I going to do it? Make my reader pick up, sample, and then enter into a reader/writer contract with me? They will buy or borrow my book because they can trust me to deliver the goods – that is give them a book they'll enjoy.

Sadly, there are no guarantees to this. Writing

is obviously creative, and like all creative arts, it doesn't always work, or the person who liked your work before doesn't now. You've only got to think about the hairdresser who made your hair look a million dollars, so you go back and they fail to work their magic second time round. (That's probably a female-based comment, but I'm sure men have also experienced good/bad haircuts from the same person.)

But there are some key elements that writers must consider – although they don't **all** necessarily need to be there in the opening. These are:

Character – readers need a character they can relate to straight away.

Hook – can be a question; something intriguing or 'unusual' in some way; interesting setting; writing that interests; or perhaps the writing itself is intriguing.

Setting – can the reader find a place – physically, geographically, historically, emotionally, psychologically – that fixes the setting for the character/action?

Some sort of question – is the book going to explore an aspect of human experience and provide a perspective?

So, let's imagine that you the writer, having made sure that all those things are in place, send your manuscript off to an agent or publisher. What can you expect?

Presuming you've done your homework, and you're only sending to someone who might at the very least have a passing interest in the sort of stuff you write, and you've made your manuscript as free from errors as you possibly can, they will still probably say 'no'. Presuming you're not someone who has sent a children's novel to an agent that deals with science fiction/fantasy; or you haven't used some weird font in 10-point; or sent a covering letter in green ink saying how much your auntie and friends loved it. So, you're as normal as any writer can be, but the agent still says 'no' and you wonder if they've even read the pages you printed so carefully, posted so carefully, and awaited their response so carefully for months.

Why don't they want it – even when they say, as *very occasionally* they do, that they loved it? Well, usually, they don't want it. Full stop. No matter what it's like. But it's still worth remembering something important:

Agents and publishers don't read manuscripts for enjoyment. Yes, they're looking for the nugget of gold, but most of the time they read in order to REJECT a manuscript, so that they can get to the bottom of the pile. The first page or couple of pages are **crucial**. To the beginner writer, this might seem harsh, but with their eyes and ears attuned, writing professionals can make a judgement on the whole from the first pages.

'If you find one line of extraneous dialogue on page one, you will likely find one line of extraneous dialogue on each page to come.' (*The First Five Pages* Noah Lukeman) In other words, if the craft isn't there on page one, it's certainly not going to be there on subsequent pages.

Openings. So difficult. So important.

P

Plot

The craft of writing is heavy with 'p' words – a positive plethora of them! Place, point of view, pacing, but I've decided to go for plot as I believe it's an essential part of successful fiction – although definitely not at the expense of **character** (see **C**).

I think human beings crave narratives. *Once upon a time* is somehow entwined with our psyche. We look for narratives in our own lives, search for connections and patterns, talk of coincidence in terms of fate. And when life fails to deliver a neatly-structured plot, we can always turn to fiction and drama for rationalisation of the random events that happen to us. Our lives are random, but we impose structures on them; fiction is structured, but the art is to make it seem random.

The nineteenth-century was the heyday of the traditional narrative: a linear structure; a beginning, middle and end; birth, life and death. The writers many of us studied at school and grew to love – Thomas Hardy, George Eliot,

Charles Dickens – wrote the 'big' novels, which spanned whole lives, generations of families, of communities.

But the modernists of the early twentieth-century changed all that. Books such as *Mrs Dalloway* explored one day in the life of a character. One day, but a day that doesn't progress steadily forward – dawn, morning, midday and so on. But circles back and forth in time and geography, memory and reflection, until the dichotomy that haunts human beings – the solidity of days, months, years, set against the ephemeral nature of human experience – becomes painfully present for the reader. Virginia Woolf sought a circular narrative: 'I want to dig out caves behind my characters', and she and her anti-narrative collaborators rejected 'plot' and the linear structures previously used in novels.

The goals of early twentieth-century writers are understandable when seen in their historical context. Woolf wrote 'About the year 1910, the world changed', and change it did. It signalled the advent of photography, mass media, advertising, psychoanalysis, mechanized warfare. The rise of electric light and internal combustion engine overturned the noisy, smelly, gas-lit, horse-drawn world those writers grew up in. The orderly, complacent, optimistic Victorian novel had nothing to say to them.

Worse than nothing: it felt like a lie. The novel was a mirror the modernists needed to break, in order to reflect their broken world. (Wiki)

One of the things they broke was plot. To the modernists, stories were a distortion of real life. In real life stories don't tie up neatly. Events don't line up in a tidy sequence and mean the same things to everybody they happen to. The writers of the time broke the clear straight lines of **causality** and chronological sequence, to make them look more like life as it's actually lived.

I'm sure that was necessary at the time to break the hold those earlier narratives had on readers' imaginations. For many years, I adored the big nineteenth-century novel, until I experienced its limitations for twentieth and now twenty first-century psyches. Now I want a mixture. I want plot; I want a sense that things happen for a reason; I want to see cause and effect in a novel – the consequences of a character's behaviour – but I also like the writer to play with time and space.

Modern sensibilities (partly thanks to cinema) can more than cope with time shifts, flashbacks and flashforwards, diversions, circular narratives. We want to experience Woolf's 'caves' behind the characters. But I think we are also driven to read on by 'plot', by the structure of cause and effect which is the backbone of a novel.

Character and plot are inextricably intertwined. Sometimes, as in thrillers, plot will take precedence; sometimes novels will be character-driven. The American writer Kurt Vonnegut says: 'I guarantee you that no modern story scheme, even plotlessness, will give a reader genuine satisfaction unless one of those old-fashioned plots is smuggled in somewhere. I don't praise plots as accurate representations of life, but as ways to keep readers reading.'

Georges Polti, a 19th century French writer described thirty-six situations that may be found in many stories, based on the list identified by Goethe who said it was originated by Italian Carlo Gozzi (1720-1806). Some of the themes and examples relate more to Polti's own time, but they still provide useful stimuli and examples of real human dilemmas.

Here are his thirty-six situations, in alphabetical order of course:
- abduction
- adultery
- all sacrificed for passion
- ambition
- an enemy loved
- conflict with a god
- crimes of love
- daring enterprise
- deliverance
- disaster
- discovery of the dishonour of loved one

- enmity of kinsman
- erroneous judgement
- falling prey to cruelty or misfortune
- fatal imprudence
- involuntary crimes of love
- killing an unrecognised kinsman
- loss of loved ones
- madness
- mistaken jealousy
- murderous adultery
- necessity of sacrificing loved ones
- obstacles to love
- obtaining
- pursuit
- recovery of a lost one
- remorse
- revenge for a crime
- revolt
- rivalry of kinsman
- rivalry of superior and inferior
- self-sacrifice for an ideal
- self-sacrifice for kindred
- supplication
- the enigma
- vengeance taken for kindred upon kindred

If a writer can mix up a few of Polti's situations in the cooking pot of plot, a compelling story should emerge.

Q

Questions

Questions are at the heart of successful fiction, from the small 'what's going to happen next' type to the big questions about human experience – what does it mean to betray someone you love? Is there such a thing as a 'good' war? Can you be in love with two people at once? What are the consequences when self-fulfilment is sacrificed for the sake of others? Questions posed by a novel can make us wonder about our own responses to life's challenges. Would we go into a burning building to rescue an unknown child? Would we give up our pursuit of dangerous sports if our wife/husband asked us to? Would we reveal the guilt of someone we love?

It's the job, then, of the fiction writer to put characters into difficult situations. To create conflict in order to challenge our characters. Characters change through conflict, and change is the fuel that drives a story to resolution. A writer must push the boundaries, continually asking the question 'what if?' What if this happened to my character? What if that happened to my character? When in doubt, a writer needs to 'up the anti' for the character.

Having got an idea for a story, created characters, and got the bones of a story on the page, a writer should try to read it as a reader would. One of the best things I got from my creative writing MA was to ask myself the question 'What's this like for the reader?' When I'm reworking a story/novel, I try to evaluate it from a reader's perspective: What and who do I care about? What has been set in motion that I want to see completed? Where is the writer taking me? Do I trust the writer to make the journey worthwhile? I can't always make the leap from writer to reader, but trying to answer the questions is important.

Fiction involves significant questions for both writers and readers. And for the majority of readers, a good read is one that is satisfying on several levels, emotionally, psychologically and intellectually. This usually involves resolution of some kind to the question that the novel has posed. That resolution doesn't need to be neatly tied up as in 'The End', 'Reader, I married him', or 'We all lived happily ever-after': such clear resolutions are not needed for contemporary fiction.

The endings of many modern novels raise as many questions as they answer. They resist closure by offering open-ended resolutions.

They provide alternative endings that tease the reader, as John Fowles did in *The French Lieutenant's Woman*. They take on Woolf's mantle and circle back and forth in time, so that the route to resolution is challenging and constantly delayed. Maggie O'Farrell's wonderful *The Vanishing Act of Esme Lennox* uses this technique to highlight the non-linear nature of human experience – the past haunts the present; the present reaches out to the future. Past, present and future interact and impinge on each other. In Sara Waters' *The Night Watchman* the idea of linear development is overturned and the story is told in reverse. The novel takes us back through the 1940s towards 1941 – to the end which is actually the beginning.

Although I enjoyed the novel, I found this ultimately depressing and unsatisfactory. Usually one sets out on a journey/novel with the hope of a rainbow at the end. It doesn't always come, but the hope takes us forward to a new place. With the end at the beginning, the journey tends to be sullied by the knowledge that it didn't end positively. Having said that, it didn't stop me appreciating the challenge of reading a story 'turned on its head'!

Overall, though, I love the experimentation. I enjoy the fact that we, as both readers and writers, can embrace traditional narratives, but also have the opportunity to experience writing that experiments; writing that questions the traditional and 'safe'; writing that refuses to allow itself to be pigeon-holed. The post postmodern age offers us a wealth of treasures. Perhaps the real **question** should be 'what next?'

R

Rejection

From an early age we experience failure and disappointment. We've met them along the way – they're success and triumph's evil twins after all, and we've all been victims of the hurt and bitterness they like to inflict. But we're encouraged to accept them, to learn from them, let them stiffen our resolve. As Kipling said: *If you can meet with Triumph and Disaster/And treat those two imposters just the same ...*

So, rejection is part of everyone's experience: the job you didn't get, the unrequited love, the promotion you were expecting which goes to someone else, the party you weren't invited to. We all know how much such rejections hurt.

However, when you're a writer, you don't opt only for a solitary life with your laptop or notebook your main companions. You also choose a life with rejection and disappointment guaranteed. You know when you're writing your novel, when your heart is bleeding onto the page that unless you're one of a lucky minority, you face round after round of rejection from agents – even if they profess to like your work.

The chances of your novel reaching a publisher's hands are slim.

When you enter a short story for a competition, you have to do so with the hope of success. But even so, you can't help thinking about the thousands who will also enter, how good some of those stories will be, how subjective the judging is, the unlikely chance of your story getting through the initial stages ... but you tell yourself these things partly to warn off rejection and disappointment. If you've imagined sufficient obstacles, the reality of not getting through will be easier to accept you tell yourself.

And maybe, just maybe, your story makes the longlist. You bite your nails to the quick; you rush to check the website, the post for details of the shortlist. The wait is unbearable. Maybe, just maybe, your story will make the shortlist. That's it – the results are up. You scan the list of names, the titles of the stories – and you're not there.

It doesn't matter how many times you read about the unexpectedly high number of entries, the quality of the writing being outstandingly high, the difficulties of choosing. The fact remains: Rejected. Rejection. It's not even a very long word, but how its three syllables hurt.

Some time ago, a piece of mine made the shortlist of a prestigious competition, one I've wanted to be successful in for ages. I couldn't help having high hopes, even though I warned myself not to. And then came the results – I hadn't made that last leap onto the winners' podium. I realised the truth of that old cliché: you *can* taste disappointment.

But then I had some email correspondence with the organiser of the competition. I'll preserve his anonymity by calling him Bearer of Bad News or BBN for short! It went like this:

******* (title of piece) *didn't make it to the last ten. Sorry. Just got the results half an hour ago.* BBN

Thanks for letting me know. I'm very disappointed, but nice to have the dream for a short time! Lindsay

Tis a bloody tough choice being a writer. My heart goes out to you. Just as it is lovely, and rewarding, telling (the few) writers that their work has made it, it is equally awful telling the ones who didn't make it. Please don't be discouraged, but keep trying and hopefully enjoying it. BBN

Thanks for this nice email. Really appreciate it. I've had quite a lot of success so far this year, so I shouldn't feel sorry for myself, but **** (competition name) holds some magic for me. I've made the short story longlist a couple of times (one of those might have been the shortlist before you changed how you did it) but never quite made it. But I'll keep trying! Lindsay

Have to say, you are one of the relatively few people who have made me feel OK for giving them bad news. Thanks. It's big of you. BBN

Those words were enough to make me dry my – metaphorical – tears and get back to the computer. *Tis a bloody tough choice being a writer.* It certainly is. But if you're driven to write – and it is a compulsion – then there is no choice: it's what you do, and rejection is the necessary price you pay.

S

Secrets, Shadows and Suspense

Secrets are often what drive novels. One of the main themes of my novel *The Piano Player's Son* is that secrets rarely die, however long they are hidden, and they will emerge at some stage with the power to poison the present and the future. Secrets are not so centre stage in *Unravelling*, but they are important in helping to form the characters and their relationships, as well as developing the plot.

Two of my favourite novels have secrets at their heart – one, *The Vanishing Act of Esme Lennox* I've mentioned before; and the other one is by Sebastian Barry and is called *The Secret Scripture*. If the revelation at the end of the latter is disappointing, the rest of the novel is so wonderful and poignant that, for once, I agree with the praise it receives, for example *powerful and memorable/A beautiful book about human frailty/The unstable nature of memory and identity is beautifully evoked.*

But even when secrets aren't the driving force,

a major reason why readers keep turning the pages is to find out what happens or how it happens or why it happens. Readers keep reading as long as there is enough suspense, so a writer needs to be aware of the importance of withholding information.

New writers sometimes struggle with knowing when to disclose information to readers, and how much to disclose when they do. It's tempting to give away too much too soon. We are used to thrillers providing a trail of clues for readers to follow. The reader grows more and more involved as various clues are dropped into the narrative. But each one leads the reader only one step closer to the truth, while building up to the key revelation. The technique doesn't apply only to thrillers and crime. Every fiction writer needs to hold back information until the last possible moment. Instead of thinking *how soon can I get this information across*? the writer needs to think *how long can I hold back from telling this?*

A useful metaphor is the jigsaw. Too difficult and it becomes frustrating; too easy and there's no point carrying on, or you race through with little sense of satisfaction. The pacing of the clues is all-important. What's left unsaid, what lurks in the shadows waiting to be revealed, is as significant (often more so) as what is said.

A technique that is often used in generating

suspense is foreshadowing. We're used to flashbacks – partly thanks to cinema – but foreshadowing can play a role as well. Foreshadowing involves planting clues, both subtle and direct, into the text to suggest things that might happen in the future.

It can add dramatic tension to the narrative, building anticipation for what is to come. A reader might not understand the clues at the time, but will inevitably try to guess what they mean. If they're right, there is a sense of satisfaction in predicting future happenings, or revelations. If they're wrong, there's the enjoyment of surprise: *Wow! I didn't see that coming.* But that will only work if the outcome is believable.

I think the best foreshadowing is when the reader picks up subtle clues (maybe without even fully realising) and then there's the wonderful shock of recognition/realisation when the revelation finally comes – that sense of *Oh, I see!*

T

Titles

The title of a book/story is something writers often struggle with. And yet, it plays a significant role when a book is trying to reach out to its potential readers. A reader might decide whether to pick up the book of a novelist they don't know, or read a short story by a writer they've never heard of, because of the title. It might just be the thing that influences them to take the novel off the shelf, or start reading that particular story in an anthology or magazine.

Creating a title is as important as any other piece in the narrative puzzle. But sometimes writers can't find an appropriate title for their work or beginning writers might say *I haven't bothered with a title yet*. But it's been said that's similar to calling your child *Hey, you* until he or she starts walking!

Titles lie at the heart of a work, shaping its identity, its personality, and hinting at its layers of meaning. David Lodge says 'The title of a novel is part of the text – the first part of it, in fact, that we encounter – and therefore has considerable power to attract and condition the reader's attention.'

For that reason, it's a good idea to avoid summary titles. If the story is about a boy called George who runs away, it's better not to call it 'George runs away' or 'George escapes'. The aim should be to let the title enhance the subtext of the work or prompt the reader to consider the story in a new light.

Sometimes titles are only the name of the main character – probably more common in titles from the past. Though this can convey something of the flavour of the novel, suggesting the power and individuality of the character, I think this sort of title lacks the intrigue that a more complex title can offer. Compare *Emma*, *Jane Eyre* or even *Anna Karenina* with *I Know Why the Caged Bird Sings*, *Light in the Snow*, *The Handmaid's Tale*. These convey more vividly the mysteries of the world inside the book's covers.

I would say the same thing hold true for novels that have place in their titles: *Mansfield Park*, *Washington Square*, *Wuthering Heights*.

Other titles point up the underlying themes of the novel: *Sense and Sensibility*, *Crime and Punishment*, *Atonement*. But I'm not sure that I want my 'take' on the book's morality forced on me so much by the title.

Titles are sometimes only one word: Rushdie's *Shame*, AL Kennedy's *Day*, Jim

Crace's *Quarantine*, Lindsay Stanberry-Flynn's *Unravelling*. If successful, these can pack an initial punch, but also reveal the subtleties the novel has to offer.

Some time ago, I remember reading that the majority of novels in the top ten best-sellers had the word 'The' in the title – and that was after I'd decided on the title *The Piano Player's Son* for the title of my next novel. Certainly, this was true on the occasions I checked the paperback novel charts. The dominance of the charts by Fifty Shades temporarily skewed those results, but even so, more often than not, the majority of top-selling books in Saturday's Guardian weekly charts will begin with the word 'The'.

It would be interesting to know what you think makes a great title. As a reader, what draws you to a title? As a writer, what do you try to achieve with your titles? Do you give them enough thought?

One title *I* particularly like is *Painter of Silence*, a novel by Georgina Harding. The title is poignant and full of possibility. It raises questions and I am drawn to its ambiguity: is the painter silent? If so, why? Is he/she painting silence? But the idea of painting silence is puzzling, and therefore intrigues me.

U

Unravelling

I wrote the first draft of *Unravelling* when I was doing my MA at Bath Spa University. I'd read an article by Christa d'Souza about going to her parents' third wedding, and I was immediately intrigued by the idea that the same two people might remarry each other other at different stages in their lives, and I started to think why?

D'Souza's father was about twelve years older than her mother, and they married for the third time when he was suffering from ill health. He had an Anglo-Indian background, and d'Souza's mother was very young at the time of their first marriage. They formed the template for *my* couple in *Unravelling* – Vanessa and Gerald. Gerald is not Anglo-Indian, but I do try to suggest an alternative, somewhat exotic background for him. Mysterious, but possibly something related to South America.

Vanessa and Gerald meet when Vanessa is eighteen and has just started at art school – which I based on Hornsey College of Art in

Crouch End, London. Gerald, is a charismatic (well, I think he is, but not everybody agrees!) talented sculptor, who teaches at the school. A rebellion occurred at Hornsey College of Art in the late 1960s, when the students and some of the tutors held a sit-in in rejection of the educational practices of the time. Gerald is part of that rebellion in *Unravelling*.

Like d'Souza's parents, Vanessa and Gerald divorce, although I wouldn't want to give away what happens to anyone who hasn't read the book, by revealing if the path of their relationship follows the same pattern as the d'Souza couple.

Vanessa's parents are Irish and her father – a domineering man – doesn't want Vanessa to go to art college, but she manages, with her mother's help, to attend, with the idea that she will have a career as an art teacher. However, teaching is far from Vanessa's mind – she wants to be a fashion designer, and is besotted with Mary Quant. She later becomes highly successful as a knitwear designer, something the younger Gerald completely disapproves of.

While I'm a writer, I can't paint, draw, sculpt (I used to knit, but not any more), but to make life more difficult for myself, these artistic talents are at the heart of *Unravelling*. I have a friend who is an artist, and she gave me a lot of help with the artistic side. Another friend makes the most wonderful knitwear. She taught me loads of stuff about modern yarns – which have moved on a long way from four-ply and double-knit! – and took me to an amazing wool shop in Shipston-on-Stour where I fell in love with almost everything I saw! People have said how evocative the knitwear descriptions in *Unravelling* are, so I think I must have pulled it off, or *cast on okay* – or whatever the appropriate metaphor is!

Christa d'Souza wrote in her article that the experiences she and her sister had of their parents' marriage had made them ambivalent about marriage itself. I wanted to explore the impact of divorce on a child, and the possible effects in later life. I created the characters Cordelia and her sister, Esme, in order to look at this. However, I quickly realised that although Vanessa and her story had come into my head almost fully formed, I hadn't thought very much about Cordelia, and I had to do a lot of work to create a credible character with a plot of her own.

As a result of her experiences, Cordelia has a difficult relationship with her mother, Vanessa. I was pleased when I heard from a book group of women, mainly in their thirties and forties, that the book had sparked an interesting discussion on daughter/mother relationships as a result of Cordelia's relationship with Vanessa. My novels and short stories all explore the complex links and discords within families, whether between parents and children, or between siblings.

Clearly, although it's a while since its publication, I still feel passionate about *Unravelling*, and I do think that a writer has to love his/her idea and the characters. If you, as their creator don't love – or feel passionate about them in some way: angry with them, hate them, desire them – then there's not much chance a reader will feel for them.

V

Voice and Viewpoint

It's important if you want to be a successful writer to create a strong voice. It doesn't always have to be the same voice – in fact it's an advantage if you can use different narrative voices to suit your material. Different voices can be achieved in various ways: through the narrative point of view you choose – the character telling the story will largely dictate the voice; through the sort of language and sentence structure you use – a terse writing style with short punchy sentences might lend itself to a thriller or adventure story, but not be the best voice for a love story; through the tone you adopt – cynical, ironic, serious, dreamy, optimistic, cocky. Point of view, use of language and tone can all contribute to a distinctive voice.

A strong narrative voice gives readers confidence in the writer. They can relax in the knowledge that the writer knows what he/she is doing. A reader and writer enter into a contract with each other. The reader trusts the writer to produce a well-written story that it is worthwhile spending time reading, and the writer implicitly declares 'I'll deliver the goods.' It is a similar experience to going to the theatre or cinema. If the actor on stage stumbles over their lines, lacks stage presence, 'feels' wrong for the character, or the film star doesn't inhabit their role convincingly, or lacks the authority to make the character authentic, the audience will be disappointed and feel let down by the failure of the film/play to fulfil the terms of the contract.

We can see an example of a strong narrative voice in Stephen King's *Carrie*: *Momma was a very big woman, and she always wore a hat. Lately her legs had begun to swell, and her feet always seemed on the point of overflowing her shoes. She wore a black cloth coat with a black fur collar. Her eyes were blue and magnified behind rimless bifocals. She always carried a large black satchel purse and in it was her change purse, her billfold (both black), a large King James Bible (also black) with her name stamped on the front in gold, and a stack of tracts secured with a rubber band.*

I think this is a strong narrator. Stephen King has chosen specific and wonderful details – I love *her feet always seemed to be on the point of overflowing her shoes* – which help create an authentic, commanding voice.

Point of view is inextricably linked with voice. If a writer chooses a first or third person narrator, or even second, or an unreliable narrator, or a detached, external narrator, the voice used will inevitably be different.

John Gardner in his book *The Art of Fiction* explains very clearly the impact of an intimate narrator versus a distant, external narrator. Essentially, his work explores the different ways in which the reader is taken, by the narrator, inside the character's head. Gardner gives us five different ways of narrating the same scene:

1. **It was winter of the year 1853. A large man stepped out of a doorway.** A completely detached narrator. One who focuses more on the year and the season than the character – we don't even discover his name. This is an observer of events, a distant narrator conveying little emotion.
2. **Henry J. Warburton had never much cared for snowstorms.** We now have the character's name. Based on a name, we can start to form impressions, make judgements. We've moved a little closer to the character.
3. **Henry hated snowstorms.** The description becomes more personal. The surname is dropped, and this is potentially someone we know, or are about to get to know. He could be a friend.
4. **God how he hated these damn snowstorms.** A much more intimate voice. It's not quite first-person, but we are close to the character, not in his head exactly, but perhaps perched on his shoulder, feeling

and hating these snowstorms as much as he is.

5. **Snow. Under your collar, down inside your shoes, freezing and plugging up your miserable soul.** This is an interesting one. We're right with the character, the snow under our collar and inside our shoes. Wet and miserable. It's an intimate description, told in the second-person. This voice can sometimes create a sense of detachment, but here, I think, it draws the reader in, so that we share the character's experience and emotions. We've moved a long way from (1) where we don't even know the character's name.

From Gardner's wonderful examples, it's easy to see how a writer can vary the intimacy or the distance of the narrative voice in the same way a film maker can manipulate the viewer's response through the focal length of the shot.

W

Write

I've written ever since I was a child. I don't know where the desire came from. I was an avid reader, but no one I knew wrote stories, except when told to at school. But I amassed exercise books and filled page after page, often with boarding school stories, or girls forced to leave home and make their own way in difficult circumstances. Even then, it seems, I understood the necessity to challenge your characters.

I say I've written since I was a child, but in fact there were long periods when I didn't write at all. Caught up with studying, then a career and raising a family, writing got squeezed out. Although that's not strictly true, as I wrote four novels when my children were small, all in long hand – something I wouldn't want to do now.

Since I started writing seriously again about thirteen years ago, I can't imagine not being able to do it. It's a passion, a compulsion that I feel driven to do even though sometimes I don't want to and it seems too hard!

At those times, I question WHY? What has planted in me this need to create characters, to make up stories, to live in imaginary worlds often more real than the world around me? Wouldn't it be more useful to have gardening, woodwork, learning a musical instrument or such like as my passion?

It was in one of those moods that I wrote the following *cri de coeur*:

To write or not to write – that is the question:
Whether tis better in life to hold parties,
To travel the world, to take up gardening,
Or to sit at the computer day after day,
And by writing, feed creativity.
To write – make up characters, plots and stories;
To live in fictional worlds more true than life.
But time – where oh where will I find the time?
Squeeze moments from my busy, frenzied day
Or stay up late, losing sleep? My much-loved sleep.
To sleep – perchance to dream – what dreams may come:
An agent, three-book deal, bestseller list,
A world-wide tour, readers eager for more.
But then, morning's here, and with it doubts and fears,
For who would bear the scorn and derision
Of the agent's letter, and the thud of rejection slips on the hallway floor?
Who would put themselves through such cruel torment,
Neglecting partners, friendships, and so much more?

But then the dread of what comes after writing:
The undiscovered country, that sterile land,
Where imagination shrinks and shrivels,
Where characters must die, their lives unlived.
No, I will not let my dreams and hopes
Grow sicklied with the pale cast of thought.
No, I will not squash my inspiration,
Turn away and lose the name of action.
The world must take its turn, for I **will** write.

I'm afraid some of the iambic pentameters don't pass muster, but WS was not above slipping in the odd nine or eleven syllables. So, who am I to quibble?

X

X-Ray

This letter was always going to be a tricky one! Try counting how many words in the dictionary beginning with x. It won't take you long!

But it's not just a cheap trick to get me out of a difficult x-shaped hole, because I think x-ray vision is what we need to apply to writing **after** the first creative burst is down on paper.

The first draft is where we can let our imagination and creativity roam free. It's important at this stage **not** to let our critical minds exert too much influence, as it can become impossible to write anything for fear of writing rubbish. Not that I always manage to take that advice: the impulse to correct, rework, polish, is so strong, that it can be hard to squash it. And sometimes, beginning the day's writing by rereading and revising the previous day's has the advantage of letting you immerse yourself in the thread of the story again.

But, generally, too much tinkering – constant stopping to rework a particular paragraph – will block progress. However, once that draft is done, it's time for the real task – rewriting, revising, editing, the minute checking of every facet of the piece.

Sometimes writers who are starting out struggle with the idea of rewriting their work. 'I've already written it,' they say. 'What's the point of doing it again?' Perhaps what they don't realise is that most professional writers write numerous drafts before their work reaches a wider audience. There might be a minority who achieve something good with their first draft, but for the majority that first burst of creativity is only the beginning of a long process.

John Fowles, most famous for his 1960s' novel *The French Lieutenant's Woman*, apparently wrote the first draft of his earlier work *The Collector* in barely a month. However, he said 'Of course a lot of it was poorly written and had to be endlessly revised or amended. First-draft and revision writing are so different they hardly seem to belong to the same activity.' And in a more succinct version of the importance of revising, Raymond Chandler, author of *The Big Sleep* and *The Long Goodbye* wrote 'Throw up into your typewriter every morning. Clean up every noon.'

So presuming you buy into the need to rewrite, rewrite, rewrite, how to go about it?

This is where our x-ray vision must come into

play. It's the moment to distance ourselves from our 'baby' and examine, probe, question with the fierce gleam of an editor/writer's eye. I can only manage this part of the process with a hard copy. Text on the screen looks different somehow from text on paper. It's easier to miss mistakes and weaknesses on the screen. Although I was discussing recently with some students how putting the text into a different font or changing the size of the font can sometimes make us look at the piece with fresh eyes. It's worth trying anything to help ourselves spot what's not working.

With their x-ray glasses on, writers have to review their work from numerous angles:

- are the characters engaging, believable, sympathetic?
- are there some saggy/slow bits or parts of the plot that don't hang together?
- is the dialogue realistic? People don't talk in beautifully crafted, coherent sentences.
- are the characters' goals clear, and do they make sense?
- do the characters' emotions come over?
- is it clear what the main character wants?
- are there repetitions, clichés, qualifiers, an outbreak of 'justs', or weakners such as 'appeared to' or 'seemed to'?
- have the three As crept in - adverbs, adjectives (sparing use acceptable), abstract words? As Stephen King in his

book *On Writing* said 'The road to hell is paved with adverbs.'
- is the writing clear, precise, economical?

The list of things to check is endless and the role of self-critic is difficult. There are a number of agencies, as well as individuals, who will offer editorial advice and feedback, but obviously these services have to be paid for. What can be invaluable for a writer is to work with a writing group. A good group will offer constructive criticism, as well as providing motivation and discipline. Critiquing other writers' work can also help writers see what works and doesn't, and why. 'In writing competitions, the work of authors who belong to writers' groups stands head and shoulders above the rest in maturity, style and construction.' (Celia Brayfield)

And a final thought from Stephen King: 'Write with the door closed; rewrite with the door open.'

Y

Yellow

One of the interesting features of the original alphabet blogging challenge was discovering the wealth of possible words, relating to an aspect of reading/writing, which begin with certain letters compared with the lack of words from other letters. And, yes, as you might have guessed, X, Y and Z have not proved to be the easiest!

However, the end is in sight, and I **will** get to the end of the alphabet – somehow or another!

So, I've chosen *yellow* because it helps illustrate how mood and atmosphere can be suggested in fiction without having to describe them – showing versus telling. Close your eyes for a moment and think about the different scenes that appear in your mind if I ask you to think about the colour *gold* and then compare it with the colour *straw*.

Imagine you are painting your new kitchen. You fancy painting it yellow. You find a shade on the paint chart described as *buttercup*. That's just right, you decide. It evokes the optimism of spring, a feeling you want to create in a room where family and friends will gather to share food and news. The colour will spread the happiness you remember from when you were a child and someone thrust a buttercup under your chin to see if its reflected light shone on the skin under your chin meaning you liked butter.

But then, your husband/wife/partner points to another shade – *mustard*. You stare at the word and you remember the walls of your classroom, the long hospital corridor you walked down to visit your father in the weeks before he died. You feel bleak and lonely.

Colour has the power to capture and convey emotion and memories, in a similar way to music and smells such as perfume. Compare acid yellow with honey, straw with canary yellow, daffodil yellow with beige. Different moods. When a writer is specific, not simply describing something as yellow (or any other colour), but homing in on the exact shade, he or she can evoke contrasting emotions in the reader. Being specific is an important element in evocative writing.

The colour yellow is also interesting in that – like red and green – it has symbolic meanings beyond its 'yellowness'. Yellow is associated with cowardice for example – think of 'yellow-bellied'.

It's a writer's job to play with such links, to

suggest, to tease. 'I think I might wear my canary yellow T-shirt this evening!' she said.

Z

Zenith

In astronomy, the word 'zenith' relates to a point in the sky directly above a given position or observer. Colloquially, it is used to describe the highest point or state, or a peak. So, it seems fitting to choose it for the last letter of this alphabet anthology. I've made it!

It's also relevant as the final stages of a novel must rise to a peak second only to the opening pages in importance. As the novel builds to its climax, readers' sense of momentum will increase. Celia Brayfield describes them as 'gasping for the final scenes'.

During the course of a novel, the main character has undertaken a journey which will have made emotional and psychological demands – possibly physical ones too, depending on the genre – and readers have shared this journey. They can sense the peak (zenith) is near, and the pace of their reading accelerates in order to reach it sooner. The pace of the narrative needs to be finely judged at this stage in order to maximise the impact of the climax.

At the climax, the focus needs to narrow, to be on one character, one story-line and the one event that will finally demonstrate the theme of the novel.

'The challenge of the ending is to create power without bulk, to write simply but with tremendous force. The emotions of the central character are a key factor to achieving this. The reader has lived the whole story on an emotional plane and is seeking a peak experience at the end, a catharsis, a complete discharge of the immense feelings which the narrative has aroused.' (Celia Brayfield)

And now, I'm off for some: **Zzzzzzzzzzzzzzz!** However, like any writer, my mind is full of new projects, so I'll bounce back soon with renewed **zest**.

Acknowledgements

My thanks to:
All those who subscribe to my blog, or dip into it from time to time; to the lovely people who suggested I turn my blog posts into a book; to Joanne Phillips for her generous and invaluable help; to Christine Steenfeldt, Polly Robinson, Lynne Powell, Derek Taylor and Maggie Cox for their encouragement; and of course to Trevor for his unfailing love, help and support.

I've referred to a number of books on creative writing in this anthology, in particular: *Nail Your Novel* Roz Morris, *The First Five Pages* and *The Plot Thickens* Noah Lukeman, *Bestseller* Celia Brayfield, *The Art of Fiction* John Gardner, *On Writing* Stephen King

I have also highlighted several novels including: *The End of the Affair* Graham Greene, *The Weather in the Streets* Rosamund Lehmann, *The Siege* and *The Betrayal* Helen Dunmore, *The Vanishing Act of Esme Lennox* Maggie O'Farrell, *The Secret Scripture* Maggie O'Farrell, *Carrie* Stephen King, *The Collector* and *The French Lieutenant's Woman* John Fowles, *The Big Sleep* and *The Long Goodbye* Raymond Chandler, *Book of Dreams* Jack Kerouac, *Frankenstein* Mary Shelley, *Metamorphosis* Franz Kafka, *The Brothers Karamazov* Dostoevsky

About the author

Lindsay Stanberry-Flynn is a novelist and short story writer. She has written two novels *Unravelling* (2010), which has won three awards, and *The Piano Player's Son* (2013). Publisher, Cinnamon Press says: *The novel is accessible, but not predictable; secrets pervade the story and are skilfully handled.* A number of Lindsay's short stories have also been published. Lindsay lives in Worcestershire with her husband and has three grown-up children.
To find out more:
www.lindsaystanberryflynn.co.uk